Annie's®

Quilted Purses & Totes

LEISURE ARTS, INC. • Maumelle, Arkansas

Each pattern in *Quilted Purses & Totes* pays close attention to detail, techniques and the current needs of both the maker and the user. Whether you make one of these projects for a friend or for yourself, you'll find everything you're looking for right here. There's a wide variety of skill levels and styles with easy-to-read instructions and diagrams. This collection of purses and totes will become your go-to book not only for ideas, but also for instruction.

ENJOY!

ANNIE'S STAFF
EDITOR **Carolyn S. Vagts**
CREATIVE DIRECTOR **Brad Snow**
PUBLISHING SERVICES DIRECTOR **Brenda Gallmeyer**
MANAGING EDITOR **Barb Sprunger**
TECHNICAL EDITOR **Angie Buckles**
COPY MANAGER **Corene Painter**
SENIOR COPY EDITOR **Emily Carter**
TECHNICAL ARTIST **Amanda Joseph**
SENIOR PRODUCTION ARTIST **Nicole Gage**
PRODUCTION ARTISTS **Glenda Chamberlain, Edith Teegarden**
PRODUCTION ASSISTANTS **Laurie Lehman, Marj Morgan, Judy Neuenschwander**
PHOTOGRAPHY SUPERVISOR **Tammy Christian**
PHOTOGRAPHY **Matthew Owen**
PHOTO STYLISTS **Tammy Liechty, Tammy Steiner**

CHIEF EXECUTIVE OFFICER **David McKee**
EXECUTIVE VICE PRESIDENT **Michele Fortune**

LEISURE ARTS STAFF
Editorial Staff
CREATIVE ART DIRECTOR **Katherine Laughlin**
PUBLICATIONS DIRECTOR **Leah Lampirez**
SPECIAL PROJECTS DIRECTOR **Susan Frantz Wiles**
PREPRESS TECHNICIAN **Stephanie Johnson**

Business Staff
PRESIDENT AND CHIEF EXECUTIVE OFFICER **Fred F. Pruss**
SENIOR VICE PRESIDENT OF OPERATIONS **Jim Dittrich**
VICE PRESIDENT OF RETAIL SALES **Martha Adams**
CHIEF FINANCIAL OFFICER **Tiffany P. Childers**
CONTROLLER **Teresa Eby**
INFORMATION TECHNOLOGY DIRECTOR **Brian Roden**
DIRECTOR OF E-COMMERCE **Mark Hawkins**
MANAGER OF E-COMMERCE **Robert Young**

Library of Congress Control Number: 2014955821
ISBN-13/EAN: 978-1-4647-3338-3
UPC: 0-28906-06445-2

PROJECTS

Quick Clutch Purse

These cute and versatile clutches are a great way to use precut 10" squares and create desirable last-minute gifts for any occasion.

Design by Jen Eskridge

Skill Level
Beginner

Finished Size
Purse Size: 9½" x 4½"

MATERIALS

- 2 fat quarters or 3 precut 10" squares
- Thread
- 20" square heavy-weight interfacing
- 12" non-separating nylon zipper
- 14mm magnetic snap
- Zipper-foot attachment
- Basic sewing tools and supplies

Project Notes: *Make an easy change to the style of your clutch purse by using a different flap pattern. Select one from the patterns given or design one of your own!*

CUTTING

From fabric:
- Cut 2 (10" x 5") rectangles from each fat quarter or from 2 (10") squares—2 for outer purse, 2 for lining.
- Cut 2 selected flap pieces as per pattern.

From interfacing:
- Cut 2 (10" x 5") rectangles.
- Cut 2 selected flap pieces as per pattern.

PREPARING THE FLAP

1. Place the two fabric flap pieces right sides together. Sandwich the fabric flap layers between two interfacing flaps and pin layers together.
2. Stitch around the sides and across the bottom, leaving the top 10" edge open as shown in Figure 1.

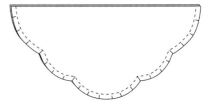

Figure 1

3. If using the curved-edge flap, clip corners and into the curve seam allowance, again referring to Figure 1.

4. Turn the stitched flap right side out, pushing curves and corners into a smooth shape using a blunt tool or eraser end of a pencil; press. Edgestitch as shown in Figure 2.

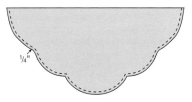

Figure 2

5. Fold the stitched flap in half and crease to mark the center. Measure in 1½" from the stitched edge and place a pin on the flap as shown in Figure 3. Slightly open the flap, and using a pencil, mark where the pin location falls on the inside of the interfacing.

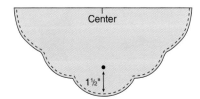

Figure 3

6. Following snap manufacturer's instructions, apply one side of the magnetic snap at the marked location, working from the inside of the flap. **Note:** *The snap prongs will go through one layer of fabric and one layer of interfacing only.*

APPLYING THE ZIPPER

1. Layer the following pieces in the order given referring to Figure 4: interfacing rectangle, outer rectangle right side up, zipper right side down and a lining rectangle right side down.

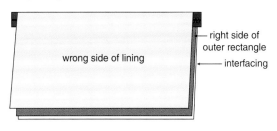

Figure 4

2. Using a zipper foot, sew along the entire length of the top edge of the layers using a ⅜" seam allowance. **Notes:** *This stitching line should be within ⅛" of the zipper teeth as shown in Figure 5. You cannot see the zipper teeth as you sew, but you will be able to feel them with your fingers.*

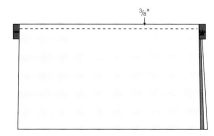

Figure 5

3. Open this unit to reveal the zipper. Fold the outer and lining rectangles away from the zipper teeth as shown in Figure 6; press.

Figure 6

4. For the remaining side of the purse, layer the pieces in the following order: interfacing rectangle, outer rectangle right side up, flap centered with snap side up, zipper unit with right side of zipper down and lining rectangle right side down.

5. Align the 10" edges and pin; sew using a ⅜" seam allowance as in step 3.

6. Open the seam and press. **Note:** *The purse will be shaped like a large rectangle with a zipper in the middle and the flap covering the zipper as shown in Figure 7.*

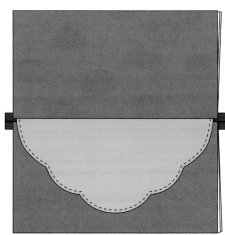

Figure 7

7. Test the zipper.
8. With a pin, mark where the flap snap falls on the purse body; apply the other side of the snap ½" above this mark and toward the zipper tape as shown in Figure 8.

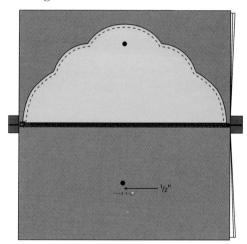

Figure 8

COMPLETING THE PURSE

1. Remove the zipper foot and apply the standard foot.
2. Unzip the zipper slightly. Apply a wide zigzag or tack stitch to the end of the zipper tape referring to Figure 9.

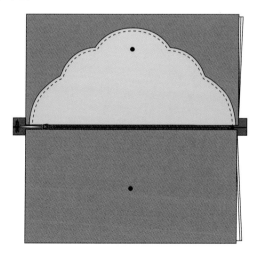

Figure 9

3. Unzip the zipper at least halfway; match the right sides of the outer rectangles to each other with the flap between. Match the right sides of the lining rectangles together. Pin around outer edges, pinning interfacing rectangles to the outer rectangles. ***Note:*** *When pinning the zipper area, be sure the zipper tape is pointed toward the lining side of the purse.*

4. Backstitching seams at beginning and end, sew around outer edges, leaving a 3" opening on the bottom edge of the lining and keeping the flap out of the way as shown in Figure 10. ***Note:*** *As you approach the zipper teeth and tape, manually roll the sewing machine's handwheel to control the needle to avoid breaking the needle.*

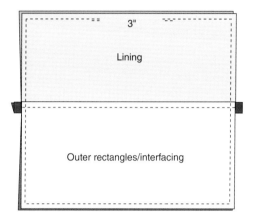

Figure 10

5. Clip corners and turn the purse right side out, pushing corners in place using the eraser end of a pencil. ***Note:*** *Trim ends of zipper even with purse edges or tuck ends into lining before turning right side out.*

6. Pull the lining up from the inside of the purse. Tuck the seam allowances into the opening and machine- or hand-sew the opening closed as shown in Figure 11. Push lining back inside to complete the purse. ●

Figure 11

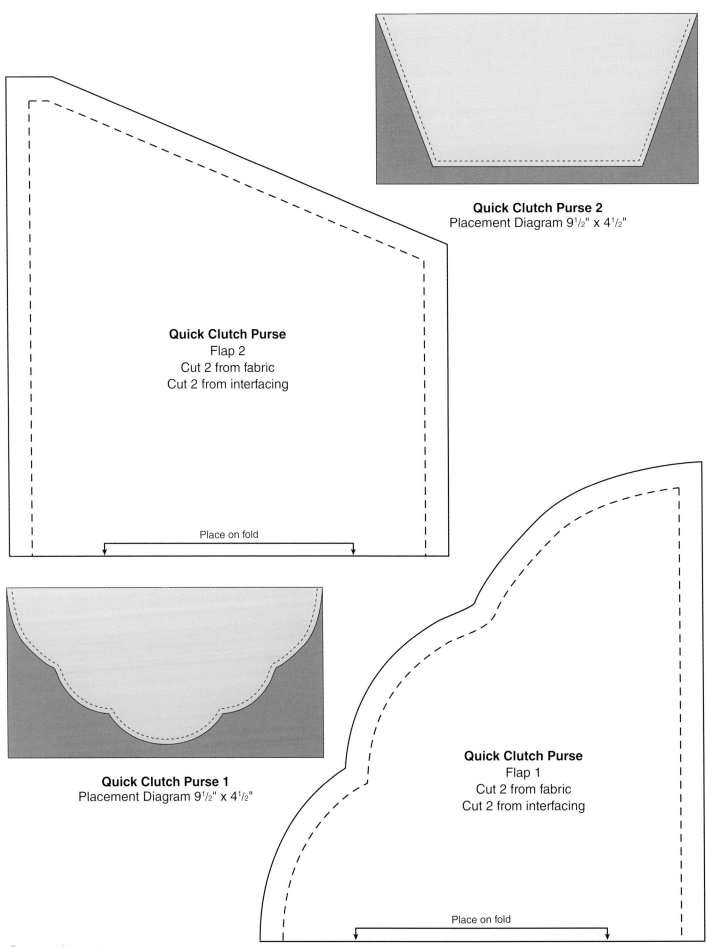

Quick Clutch Purse 2
Placement Diagram 9$\frac{1}{2}$" x 4$\frac{1}{2}$"

Quick Clutch Purse
Flap 2
Cut 2 from fabric
Cut 2 from interfacing

Place on fold

Quick Clutch Purse 1
Placement Diagram 9$\frac{1}{2}$" x 4$\frac{1}{2}$"

Quick Clutch Purse
Flap 1
Cut 2 from fabric
Cut 2 from interfacing

Place on fold

Poppy Purse

Easy-to-stitch wool will have you fashionably parading about town before you know it. Prepare yourself—you're going to get compliments on this purse!

Design by Carolyn S. Vagts for The Village Pattern Company

Skill Level
Beginner

Finished Size
Purse Size: 12" x 10" (excluding handles)

MATERIALS

- 6" square black wool felt
- 12" square red wool felt
- 12" square dark coral wool felt
- ½ yard slate blue wool felt
- ⅞ yard gray/blue cotton print
- Thread
- Pearl cotton: red, dark coral, black, yellow and lime green
- 16 (7mm) red beads
- 2 (8¼" x 5") black plastic handles
- Freezer paper
- Water-erasable marker
- Basic sewing tools and supplies

CUTTING

From slate blue wool felt:
- Cut 1 (12½" x 36") strip.
  Subcut 2 (10½" x 12½") A rectangles and 2 (1¼" x 12½") strips.

From gray/blue cotton print:
- Cut 2 (12½" x 36") strips.
  Subcut 2 (10½" x 12½") lining rectangles, 2 (1¼" x 12½") lining strips and 2 (11" x 12½") pocket rectangles.

PREPARING THE APPLIQUÉ

1. Using appliqué patterns on pages 14 and 15, trace the flower shapes onto the unwaxed side of freezer paper. Cut out shapes on traced lines. Iron each shape, waxy side down, onto the right side of the red, black and dark coral wool-felt squares as indicated on appliqué patterns. Cut around ironed shapes to create appliqué pieces; remove freezer paper.

2. Arrange and baste the flower shapes on the 10½" x 12½" A rectangles in numerical order referring to Figure 1. **Note:** *The flower design wraps around from back to front, so the pieces should align at the edges of the rectangles.*

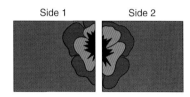

Side 1   Side 2

Figure 1

3. Hand-appliqué pieces in place using a blanket stitch and pearl cotton to match fabrics.

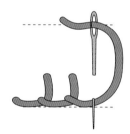

Blanket Stitch

COMPLETING THE PURSE

1. Using yellow pearl cotton, add French knots to the black flower centers as desired.

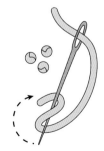

French Knot

2. Transfer the stitching pattern given to each appliquéd A rectangle.

3. Using lime green pearl cotton and a chain stitch, stitch along marked lines on each appliquéd A rectangle.

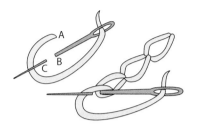

Chain Stitch

4. Sew the 7mm red beads along the stitched design to finish the outer bag pieces referring to pattern for positioning.

5. Place a 1¼" x 12½" lining strip right sides together with a same-size slate blue wool strip; stitch along both long sides. Turn right side out and press edges flat with a steam iron. Repeat with the second set of strips.

6. Subcut the stitched strips into four 5" lengths for handle tabs. **Note:** *If your handles require a different type of attachment or different-length strips, adjust the size of these strips as necessary.*

7. Measure in 2" from each end of the top edge of each outer bag rectangle; mark with a pin as shown in Figure 2.

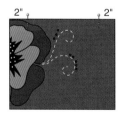

2"   2"

Figure 2

8. Insert a handle tab into each slot on each handle with the wool side out as shown in Figure 3; pin raw ends together to hold.

Figure 3

9. Pin and machine-stitch each handle tab in place at the 2" pin-marked location on the right side of each outer bag piece as shown in Figure 4.

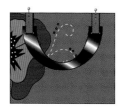

Figure 4

10. Place the two outer bag pieces right sides together with handles tucked inside; sew together on sides and across the bottom as shown in Figure 5. *Note: Be sure that the poppy halves align before stitching.*

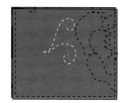

Figure 5

11. Fold each of the 12½" x 11" pocket rectangles in half with right sides together so they measure 5½" x 12½"; sew along the 12½" raw edges as shown in Figure 6. Turn right side out and press edges flat.

Figure 6

12. Place a pocket piece on the right side of each 12½" x 10½" lining rectangle 2" up from the bottom edge as shown in Figure 7. Using a ruler and a water-erasable marker, divide pocket into sections, again referring to Figure 7 or as desired to fit personal needs.

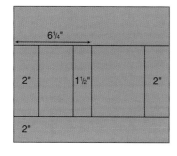

Figure 7

13. Stitch pockets in place on each end, across the bottom and on each marked line.
14. Place the two lining/pocket units right sides together and stitch sides and across the bottom, leaving a 6" opening in the bottom seam as shown in Figure 8.

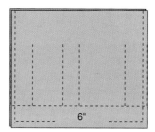

Figure 8

15. To create a flat bottom in the lining unit, match the side seam with the bottom seam; stitch across the corner 1" from the point as shown in Figure 9; trim excess ¼" from stitching line. Repeat on both bottom corners.

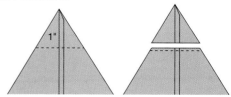

Figure 9

16. Repeat step 15 with the wool outer bag unit.
17. Slip the outer bag unit inside the lining unit with right sides together and side seams aligned as shown in Figure 10. Stitch around the top edge. *Note: The lining unit will be wrong side out; handles will be inside between the layers.*

Figure 10

18. Turn right side out through the opening in the lining, being careful with handles when turning.

19. Hand-stitch lining opening closed; press flat. Press top edge flat.
20. Topstitch around the top edge of the bag ¼" from the edge as shown in Figure 11 to finish. ●

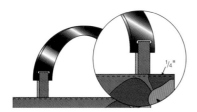

Figure 11

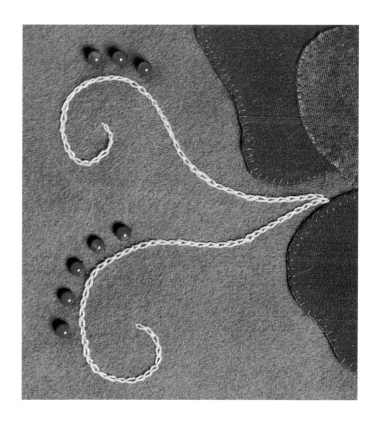

Poppy Purse Side 1
Placement Diagram 12" x 10" (excluding handles)

Poppy Purse Side 2
Placement Diagram 12" x 10" (excluding handles)

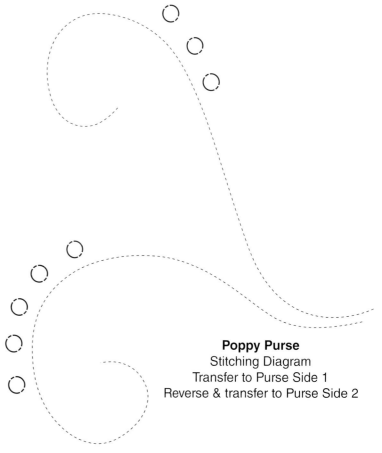

Poppy Purse
Stitching Diagram
Transfer to Purse Side 1
Reverse & transfer to Purse Side 2

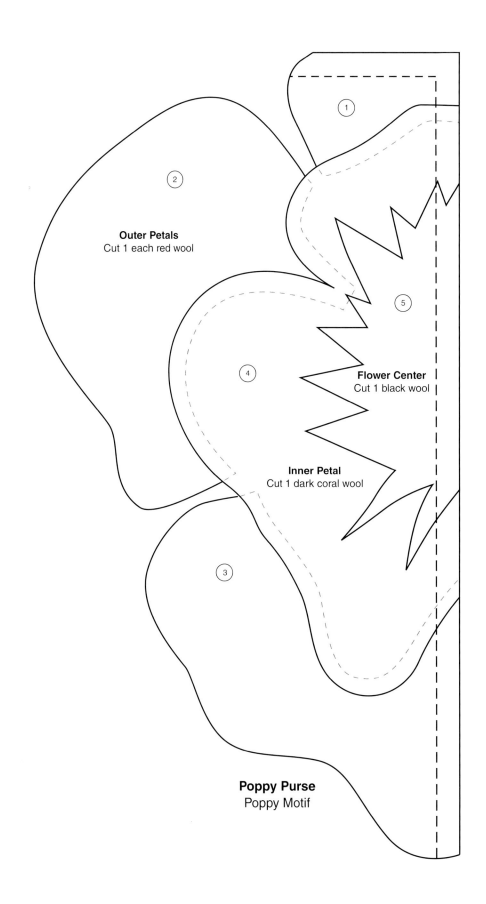

②

Outer Petals
Cut 1 each red wool

①

⑤

④

Flower Center
Cut 1 black wool

Inner Petal
Cut 1 dark coral wool

③

Poppy Purse
Poppy Motif

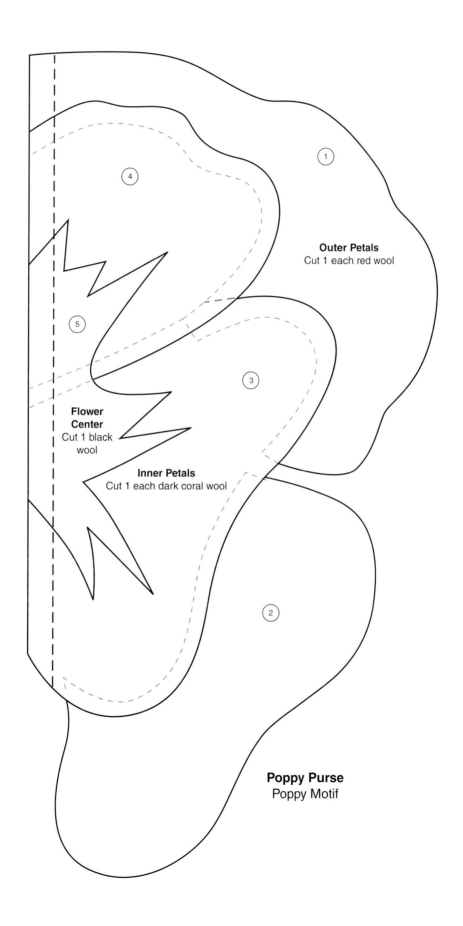

Outer Petals
Cut 1 each red wool

Flower Center
Cut 1 black wool

Inner Petals
Cut 1 each dark coral wool

Poppy Purse
Poppy Motif

Evergreen Business Tote

Go beyond the basic black with this briefcase alternative.
Ours has plenty of pockets and a laptop divider.

Design by Connie Kauffman

Skill Level
Intermediate

Finished Size
Tote Size: 14" x 13" x 3" (excluding handles)

MATERIALS

- Scraps medium and dark green prints
- ⅛ yard green tonal
- ⅜ yard dark brown tonal
- ⅜ yard tan tonal
- 1¼ yards light brown tonal
- 1⅜ yards medium brown tonal
- Batting: 19" x 23" and 19" x 31"
- Thread
- 3½ yards ¾"-wide non-roll elastic
- 1⅔ yards 22"-wide stiff fusible interfacing
- Basic sewing tools and supplies

CUTTING

From scraps medium and dark green prints:
- Cut 52 (2⅜") E squares.

From green tonal:
- Cut 1 (2¼" by fabric width) strip.
    Subcut 2 (2¼" x 17½") pocket binding strips.

From dark brown tonal:
- Cut 1 (9½" x 17½") C strip.

From tan tonal:
- Cut 3 (2½" by fabric width) A strips.
- Cut 1 (1½" by fabric width) strip.
    Subcut 4 (1½" x 6½") B strips.

From light brown tonal:
- Cut 1 (22½" by fabric width) strip.
    Subcut 2 (22½" x 14½") inner pockets.
- Cut 1 (17½" x 29½") lining rectangle.

From medium brown:
- Cut 2 (2⅜" by fabric width) strips.
    Subcut 28 (2⅜") D squares.
- Cut 1 (19" by fabric width) rectangle.
    Subcut 1 (19" x 23") F rectangle and 1 (10")
    G square.
- Cut 1 (17½" x 29½") H rectangle.
- Cut 1 (2¼" by fabric width) binding strip.

CREATING THE PATCHWORK PANELS

1. Draw a diagonal line from corner to corner on the wrong side of each D and 12 E squares.
2. Pair a D square right sides together with an unmarked E square; stitch ¼" on each side of the marked line as shown in Figure 1.

Figure 1

3. Cut apart on the marked line to make two D-E units as shown in Figure 2; press seams toward D.

Figure 2

4. Repeat steps 2 and 3 to make 56 D-E units and 24 E-E units referring to Figure 3.

Figure 3

5. Arrange and join four D-E units to make a row as shown in Figure 4; repeat to make four rows. Press seams in adjacent rows in opposite directions.

Figure 4

6. Arrange and join the D-E rows to complete a center unit as shown in Figure 5; press seams in one direction.

Figure 5

7. Repeat steps 5 and 6 to complete a second center unit.
8. Arrange and join six D-E units with six E-E units in four rows of three units each as shown in Figure 6; press seams in adjacent rows in opposite directions.

Figure 6

9. Arrange and join the D-E rows to make a side unit as shown in Figure 7; press seams in one direction.

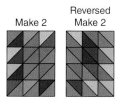

Figure 7

10. Repeat steps 8 and 9 to complete a second side unit and two reversed side units, again referring to Figure 7.
11. Sew a B strip to opposite sides of a center unit as shown in Figure 8; press seams toward B strips.

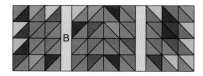

Figure 8

12. Sew a side unit and a reversed side unit to opposite sides of the B/center unit to complete one pieced panel, again referring to Figure 8; press seam toward B strips.
13. Repeat steps 11 and 12 to complete a second pieced panel.

COMPLETING THE STRAPS

1. Join the three A strips on short ends to make one long strip; press seams open.
2. Cut the elastic the same length as the joined A strip.
3. Join the short ends of the A strip to make a tube; press seam open. Repeat with the elastic.
4. Press under ¼" along one long edge of the A strip.
5. Lay the A strip right side down on a flat surface and center the elastic on top; fold the unpressed edge of A over the elastic, and then fold the pressed edge of A over this edge to cover the elastic, pinning as you continue around the tube as shown in Figure 9.

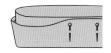

Figure 9

6. Topstitch close to the edges along the strap tube, catching the folded edge and securing the elastic as shown in Figure 10.

Figure 10

COMPLETING THE TOTE SHELL

1. Join the two pieced panels with C to complete the pocket panel as shown in Figure 11; press seams toward C.

Figure 11

2. Layer, quilt and bind the two pieced ends of the pocket panel using the 19" x 23" F piece and batting rectangle, and the 2¼" x 17½" binding strips referring to Quilting Basics on page 62. **Note:** *The pocket on the sample was quilted in the ditch of the half-square triangles to accentuate the shapes.*

3. Center the 17½" x 29½" H piece right side up on the 19" x 31" batting piece; quilt as desired by hand or machine. **Note:** *The sample was machine-quilted in a 2" diagonal grid to complement the squares in the pocket area.* When quilting is complete, trim edges even.

4. Fold the quilted H piece in half along the 29" length and crease to mark the center; repeat with the pocket panel.

5. Center the quilted pocket panel right side up on the right side of H as shown in Figure 12.

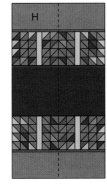

Figure 12

6. Center and pin the stitched strap over the B strips on the pocket panel. **Note:** *Measure the strap extensions at each end of the pocket panel and adjust to the exact same size for the carrying handle.*

7. Stitch strap edges in place along both edges, stitching on top of the previous stitching lines on the strip, stopping stitching 1" from the top edge at each end as shown in Figure 13 and securing stitching at the beginning and end.

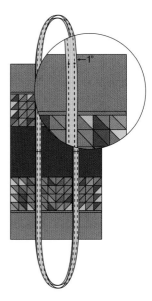

Figure 13

8. Fold the quilted tote shell with right sides together and stitch along side edges.

9. Fold each side seam flat and sew 1½" up from tip to make a square corner as shown in Figure 14. Tack the tip of the corner to the bottom of the shell, if desired.

Figure 14

COMPLETING THE TOTE

1. Cut two 11" x 14½" pieces stiff fusible interfacing. Fuse to the wrong side of one half of each 22½" x 14½" inner pocket rectangle as shown in Figure 15.

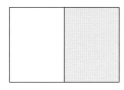

Figure 15

2. Fold the second half of the pocket rectangles over the other side of the interfacing and press.

3. Lay both sections with raw edges together—folded edges at the top; sew around side and bottom edges. Zigzag-stitch along bottom edge to complete the inner pocket.

4. Cut one 17½" x 29½" piece stiff fusible interfacing. Fuse to the wrong side of the 17½" x 29½" lining rectangle.

5. Fold the 10" x 10" G square in half with right sides together; stitch around raw edges, leaving a 3" opening on one side for turning.

6. Turn right side out through opening; press flat. Turn opening edges to the inside and hand- or machine-stitch closed to complete the inside pocket.

7. Center and pin the pocket 3½" from the top edge on the right side of the fused lining rectangle as shown in Figure 16; stitch around three sides ¼" from edge. Measure in 1½" from one side and stitch to make pocket separations.

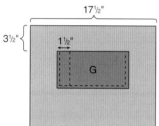

Figure 16

8. Fold the lining rectangle in half with right sides together to make a 17½" x 14¾" unit; insert the inner pocket rectangle between the layers with open side up and 1½" below the top edge with side edges extending ¼" on each side as shown in Figure 17; stitch down both sides. Trim excess fabric at ends. *Note: The inner pocket is not as wide as the folded lining so the lining will be full between the edges.*

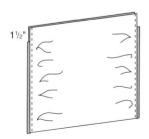

Figure 17

9. Make a square corner in the lining section as in step 9 of Completing the Tote Shell, keeping the inner pocket out of the stitching. Trim ¼" from stitching line to reduce bulk.

10. Insert lining inside the tote shell with wrong sides together, aligning side seams and top edge, poking lining all the way to the bottom of the tote shell. Trim excess lining at the top edge even with tote shell if necessary.

11. Prepare binding and bind around the top edge of the tote using medium brown binding strip referring Quilting Basics on page 62 for binding instructions. ●

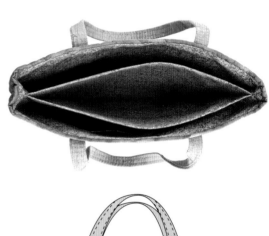

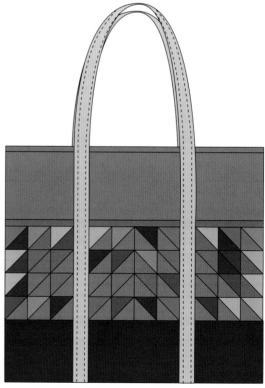

Evergreen Business Tote
Placement Diagram 14" x 13" x 3"

Orange Blossoms at the Cabin

Traditional Log Cabin blocks and fusible appliqué make a great over-the-shoulder bag.

Design by Carolyn S. Vagts for The Village Pattern Company

Skill Level
Intermediate

Finished Size
Bag Size: 16" x 14" x 4"
Block Size: 16" x 14" finished
Number of Blocks: 2

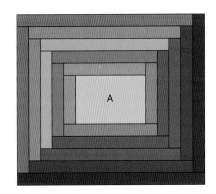

Log Cabin
16" x 14" Finished Block
Make 2

MATERIALS

- Scraps purple and red tonals or batiks
- ⅛ yard each 5 medium and 5 dark autumn-colored batiks
- 1 fat eighth each orange, yellow and green tonals or batiks
- 1¾ yards coordinating dark batik
- 1 crib-size batting
- All-purpose thread to match fabrics
- Green all-purpose thread
- ½ yard fusible web
- 2 (1¼") round coordinating buttons
- Water-soluble marker
- 1 gold magnetic snap
- Basic sewing tools and supplies

CUTTING

Trace appliqué shapes, given on pages 27 and 29, onto the paper side of the fusible web as directed on patterns for number to cut, leaving space between shapes for cutting.

Cut out shapes, leaving a margin around each one. Fuse shapes to the wrong side of fabrics as directed on each piece; cut out shapes on traced lines. Remove paper backing.

From yellow tonal or batik:
- Cut 2 (4½" x 6½") A rectangles.

From medium and dark autumn-colored batiks:
- Cut 2 (1½" by fabric width) strips from each.

From dark batik:

- Cut 4 (14½" x 4½") rectangles for purse and lining side gusset pieces.
- Cut 2 (16½" x 14½") rectangles from lining fabric.
- Cut 2 (4½" x 16½") rectangles from lining fabric for purse bottom and lining bottom.
- Cut 2 (5½" by fabric width) strips from lining fabric for handles.
- Cut 1 (12½" x 16½") rectangle from lining fabric for inside pockets.

From batting:

- Cut 2 (2" x 40") batting strips from one end of the batting.

  Set aside remainder of batting for purse body, sides and front tabs. Prepare templates for tabs and flap using patterns given; cut as directed on each piece.

COMPLETING THE BLOCKS

1. To complete one Log Cabin block, place the lightest 1½" fabric width strip right sides together on top of a 4½" end of A and stitch as shown in Figure 1.

Figure 1

2. Trim the strip even with A as shown in Figure 2; press the strip to the right side with seam toward the strip.

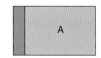

Figure 2

3. Repeat steps 1 and 2 with the same fabric strip on the top of the stitched A unit referring to Figure 3.

Figure 3

4. Repeat steps 1 and 2 with the lightest dark strip on the opposite 4½" end of A, and then on the remaining long edge of A to complete one round of strips on the A rectangle as shown in Figure 4.

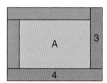

Figure 4

5. Continue adding strips around the A rectangle in numerical order, using strips in light to darkest order until you have five lights on two adjacent sides and five darks on the remaining sides to complete one block as shown in Figure 5.

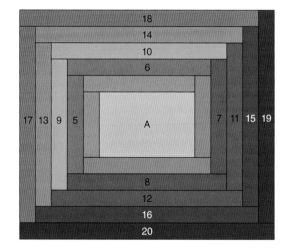

Figure 5

6. Repeat steps 1–5 to complete a second Log Cabin block.

COMPLETING THE OUTER BAG SHELL

1. Using the full-size pattern given and the water-soluble marker, draw the leaf vine onto one completed Log Cabin block referring to Figure 6 and Placement Diagram for positioning.

Figure 6

2. Stitch on the marked lines to make leaf stems using green thread.

3. Arrange and fuse a leaf and flower motif in numerical order on the Log Cabin block with the stitched stems, again referring to Figure 6 and Placement Diagram for positioning.

4. Straight-stitch around each fused shape with thread to match fabrics.

5. Join the dark bottom edges of the two Log Cabin blocks with one of the 16½" x 4½" rectangles as shown in Figure 7; press seams open.

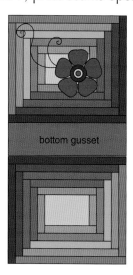

Figure 7

6. Sew one of the 14½" x 4½" rectangles with right sides together on each end of the appliquéd Log Cabin block, stopping stitching ¼" from the end of the seam as shown in Figure 8.

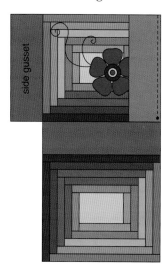

Figure 8

7. Lay the stitched outer bag shell pieces right side up on one end of the batting; trim the batting 1" larger all around.

8. Quilt as desired.

9. Place two side tab pieces right sides together on top of a matching batting piece; stitch around three sides, leaving the end open for turning. Trim batting close to stitching; clip corners. Turn right side out; press edges flat. Repeat to make a second side tab and one top flap.

10. If using a magnetic snap closure on the flap, now is the time to install it referring to the manufacturer's instructions. If using a buttonhole and button, now is the time to make the buttonhole in the flap where desired.

11. Fold and press each 5½"-wide handle strip in half lengthwise; unfold. Fold in ½" along one long edge of each 5½"-wide handle strip.

12. Center a 2" x 40" batting strip down the pressed center of each strip and baste through the center to hold in place as shown in Figure 9.

Figure 9

13. Fold the long pressed edges over the batting, with pressed edge over raw edge, and stitch in place as shown in Figure 10; remove basting. Topstitch ¼" from each long edge to finish handles. *Note: You may adjust the length of the handles to a shorter length at this time, if desired.*

Figure 10

14. Join the back and front bag panels with the side strips as in step 6. The bag bottom strip ends will still be loose; press seams to one side.

15. Sew the bottom strip ends to both side panels, stopping stitching ¼" from the ends of each seam.

16. Turn right side out to complete the outer bag shell.

COMPLETING THE BAG

1. Fold the 12½" x 16½" pocket rectangle in half right sides out so it measures 6¼" x 16½"; press.
2. Place the folded pocket rectangle on one of the 16½" x 14½" lining rectangles with the open end at least 4" from the bottom edge of the rectangle; stitch across the open end of the folded pocket rectangle referring to Figure 11. **Note:** *The folded pocket section will extend 2¼" beyond the lining piece at the bottom.* Again referring to Figure 11, fold up the pocket rectangle, press flat and pin side edges in place. Measure and mark desired pocket sections. Stitch from top to bottom of the folded pocket to create the pocket sections.

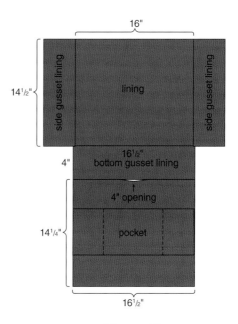

Figure 12

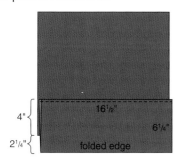

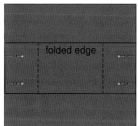

Figure 11

3. Assemble the lining in the same manner as the outer bag shell, except leave a 4" opening in the center of one of the seams when stitching the bottom rectangle to the lining front or back as shown in Figure 12.

4. Fold the unstitched ends of each side tab under ¼" and press. Position a side tab in place 3" down from the top edge with widest point toward the bottom, and with the straight edge 1" beyond seam between the side and back pieces as shown in Figure 13. **Note:** *The ¼" turned edge will be enclosed between the outer bag shell and tab.* Stitch a square shape all around the 1" area to secure as shown in Figure 14. Repeat on the opposite side with the second tab.

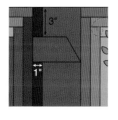

Figure 13

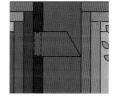

Figure 14

5. Position, pin and machine-baste the ends of one handle piece on the outer shell front 2" in from the side seams as shown in Figure 15; repeat on the outer shell back with the second handle.

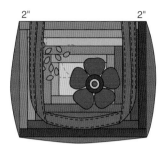

Figure 15

6. Center, pin and baste the front flap between the handles on the outer shell back as shown in Figure 16.

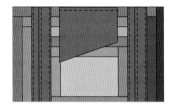

Figure 16

7. Place the outer bag shell inside the lining with right sides together, aligning seams and keeping handles inside and out of the way. Stitch around the top edge as shown in Figure 17.

Figure 17

8. Turn right side out through opening left in the bottom of the lining; turn opening edges to the inside and hand- or machine-stitch the opening closed.

9. Press around the top edge; topstitch ¼" from edge.

10. Bring the side tabs around to the front of the purse and attach with the button. ***Note:*** *The tabs should be pulled tight so that it pleats the sides and creates a less-square look. On the sample, the angled end of the tab aligns with one of the fabric strips in the Log Cabin block.* ●

Orange Blossoms at the Cabin
Placement Diagram 16" x 14" x 4"

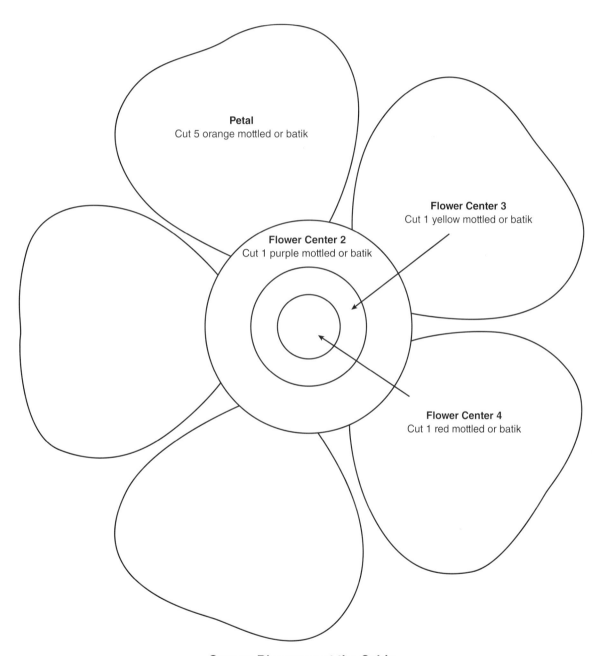

Petal
Cut 5 orange mottled or batik

Flower Center 3
Cut 1 yellow mottled or batik

Flower Center 2
Cut 1 purple mottled or batik

Flower Center 4
Cut 1 red mottled or batik

Orange Blossoms at the Cabin
Flower Appliqué Motif

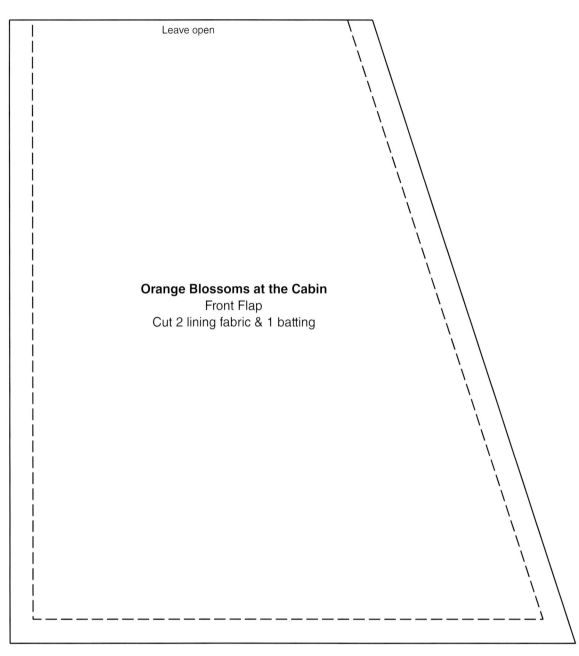

Leave open

Orange Blossoms at the Cabin
Front Flap
Cut 2 lining fabric & 1 batting

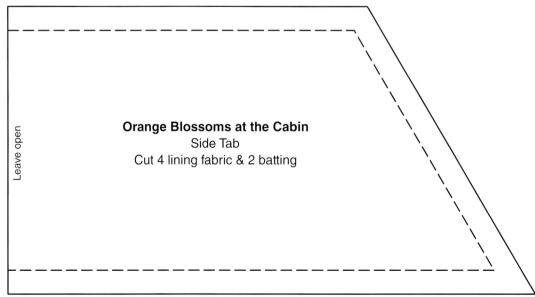

Leave open

Orange Blossoms at the Cabin
Side Tab
Cut 4 lining fabric & 2 batting

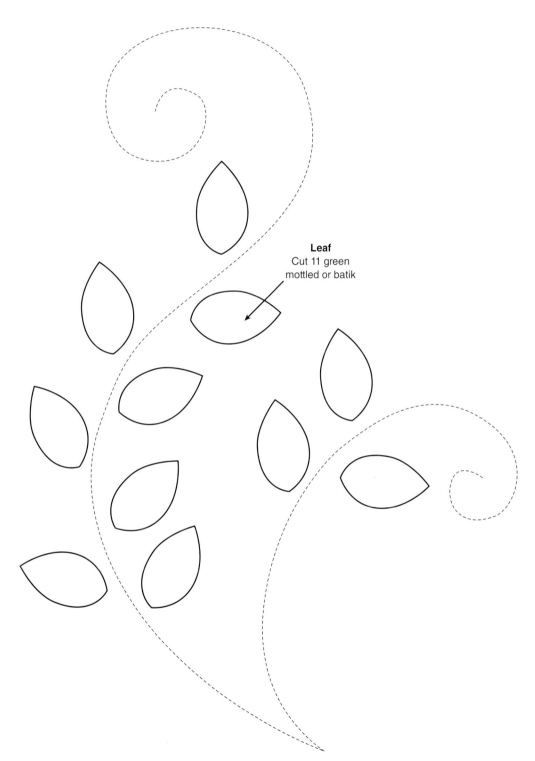

Leaf
Cut 11 green
mottled or batik

Orange Blossoms at the Cabin
Leaf Appliqué Motif

Flower Pop Tote

Make a tote that says you're ready for spring with simple construction and bright colors. Every quilter should have at least one of these.

Design by Tricia Lynn Maloney

Skill Level
Intermediate

Finished Size
Tote Size: 10" x 12" x 4" (excluding straps)

MATERIALS

- Scrap orange-with-white dots
- 1 fat quarter each:
  - orange solid
  - red-, yellow-, blue- and green-with-white dots
  - black-and-white chevron
  - white multi-dot
- ½ yard coordinating lining fabric
- Thread
- 1 yard medium-weight fusible interfacing
- Large hair elastic
- 2 (1") round orange buttons or cover buttons
- Hot-glue gun
- Basic sewing tools and supplies

CUTTING

From orange solid:
- Prepare flower circle templates using patterns given; cut as directed on each piece.

From red-with-white dots:
- Cut 1 (7½" x 21") strip.
  Subcut strip into 4 (4½" x 7½") A rectangles.
- Cut 1 (9" x 21") strip.
  Subcut strip into 4 (5" x 9") pocket rectangles.

From yellow-, blue- and green-with-white dots:
- Cut 1 (2½" x 21") B strip each fabric.

From black-and-white chevron:
- Cut 2 (2½" x 21") strips.
  Subcut strips into 2 (2½" x 14½") C strips.
- Cut 2 (3½" x 21") E strips.

From white multi-dot:
- Cut 2 (3½" x 21") strips.
  Subcut strips into 2 (3½" x 14½") D strips.

From coordinating lining fabric:
- Cut 1 (12½" by fabric width) strip.
  Subcut strip into 2 (12½" x 14½") lining rectangles.

From medium-weight fusible interfacing:
- Cut 2 (12½" x 14½") rectangles for bag body.
- Cut 2 (3½" x 21") strips for straps.

ASSEMBLY

1. Join the blue, green and yellow B strips along the 21" sides in that order to make a B strip set; press.
2. Subcut the B strip set into two 6½" x 7½" B segments as shown in Figure 1.

Figure 1

3. Sew an A rectangle to each 7½" side of each B segment to make two bag bottoms referring to Figure 2; press seams toward A.

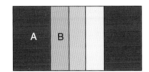

Figure 2

4. Sew a C strip to a D strip along the long edge and add to one long edge of a bag bottom to complete the front panel referring to Figure 3; press seams toward the strips. Repeat to make the back panel.

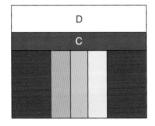

Figure 3

5. Fuse a 12½" x 14½" medium-weight interfacing rectangle to the wrong side of the front and back panels.
6. Cut a 2¼" square from each A corner of the front and back panels as shown in Figure 4.

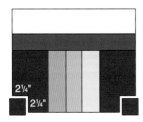

Figure 4

7. Place the front and back panels right sides together, matching edges. Stitch side and bottom seams as shown in Figure 5. Press seams open.

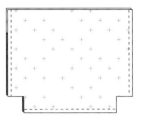

Figure 5

8. Fold bag to match bottom and side seams at cutout corners and stitch as shown in Figure 6 to make square corners and the bag bottom.

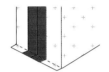

Figure 6

9. Turn the bag body right side out.
10. Place two 5" x 9" pocket rectangles right sides together and stitch all around, leaving a 3" opening on one long side referring to Figure 7. Repeat with second set of rectangles.

Figure 7

11. Clip corners and turn pockets right side out through the openings; press edges flat. Stitch opening closed.
12. Topstitch ⅛" away from the edge on the long side without the stitched opening to secure the pocket top.
13. Center a pocket on a 12½" x 14½" lining rectangle; stitch sides and bottom close to edges. Divide pocket as desired and stitch line(s) from top to bottom to make division(s) as shown in Figure 8. Repeat with second pocket and lining rectangle.

Figure 8

14. Layer the lining rectangles right sides together and repeat steps 6–8 to complete the bag lining, leaving a 7" opening in the bottom of the bag lining for turning right side out later.

15. Fuse an interfacing strip to the wrong side of each 3½" x 21" E strip.

16. Fold the long edges of each strip to the center, and then fold in half again, enclosing the raw edges inside the straps. Edgestitch along both long edges to complete the straps referring to Figure 9.

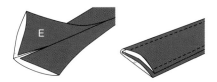

Figure 9

17. Pin and baste the ends of one strap to one top edge of the front panel 3½" from side seams as shown in Figure 10; repeat with the second strap on top edge of back panel.

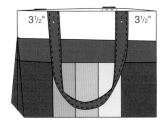

Figure 10

18. Using thread to match the hair elastic, stitch the center of the elastic loop closed to about 1" from one end of the loop as shown in Figure 11.

Figure 11

19. Center, pin and baste the elastic loop to the top of the back panel as shown in Figure 12.

Figure 12

20. Place the outer bag inside the bag lining with right sides together; stitch around the top edge as shown in Figure 13.

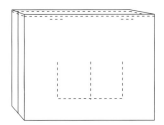

Figure 13

21. Turn the bag right side out through the opening left in the bottom of the lining; stitch the opening closed. Poke lining inside the bag, matching corners to smooth. Pull straps and elastic loop up away from bag top edges.

22. Topstitch close to the top edge.

23. Center and stitch a button on the bag front 2¼" down from the top edge as shown in Figure 14. *Note: If using cover buttons, cover with orange solid referring to manufacturer's instructions.*

Figure 14

24. Cut the five 5" orange solid circles in half and layer two halves right sides together; repeat with the 3" orange-with-white dot circles.

25. Sew each set of cut circles together along the curved edges; turn right side out and press edges smooth and flat referring to Figure 15.

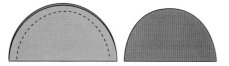

Figure 15

26. Sew a line of hand-gathering stitches along the bottom straight edge of one large stitched half circle and pull to gather as shown in Figure 16.

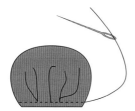

Figure 16

27. Without breaking the thread, add a second large half circle and gather as in step 25 referring to Figure 17.

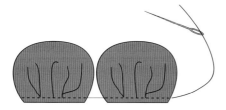

Figure 17

28. Continue adding and gathering the large half circles until all five have been gathered on the thread; pull thread tight and tie off to make the large flower as shown in Figure 18.

Figure 18

29. Repeat steps 26–28 with the three small half circles to make a small flower.
30. Layer the small flower on the large flower and secure layers together with a few hidden stitches or use a hot-glue gun.
31. Place the remaining button through the center opening in the flower and sew to the back side of the elastic loop, securing the fabric flower. Secure with hot glue, if desired.
32. Close loop over button on bag front to close the top of the bag to use. ●

Flower Pop Tote
Placement Diagram 10" x 12" x 4" (excluding straps)

Flower Pop Tote
3" Flower Circle
Cut 3 orange-with-white dots

Flower Pop Tote
5" Flower Circle
Cut 5 orange solid

Hippy Swing Bag

It's the perfect summer bag, complete with fun ruffles and a long strap for wearing across the body.

Design by Tricia Lynn Maloney

Skill Level
Intermediate

Finished Size
Bag Size: 9¼" x 11⅝" x 2" (excluding strap)

MATERIALS

- ½ yard large print
- ⅞ yard accent fabric 2
- 1 yard accent fabric 1
- Thread to match fabrics
- Interfacing 18" x 58"
- Basic sewing tools and supplies

CUTTING

From large print:
- Cut 3 (12" x 13") C rectangles for bag back and lining.

From accent fabric 2:
- Cut 2 (5" x 12") inside pocket rectangles.
- Cut 2 (5½" by fabric width) strap strips.
- Cut four (3¾" x 12) A strips.
- Cut 1 (3" x 23") top binding strip.

From accent fabric 1:
- Cut 4 (7½" x 30") B ruffle strips.

From interfacing:
- Cut 2 (12" x 13") rectangles.
- Cut 1 (1¼" x 50") strap strip.

COMPLETING THE BAG FRONT

1. Fold each B ruffle strip in half with wrong sides together along the length; press.
2. Sew two lines of gathering stitches close together along the doubled raw edge of each strip as shown in Figure 1.

Figure 1

3. Select one of these strips and stitch on each short end as in step 2 and as shown in Figure 2.

Figure 2

4. Pull the bobbin thread in each of the stitched strips to gather to make 12"-long strips as shown in Figure 3.

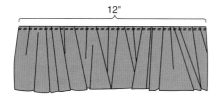

Figure 3

5. Gather the short ends of the one strip with gathering stitches at the ends to 2¼" as shown in Figure 4.

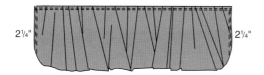

Figure 4

6. Place an A rectangle right side up on top of the 12" x 13" interfacing rectangle as shown in Figure 5; baste in place around edges.

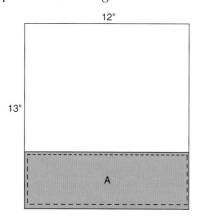

Figure 5

7. Cut a 1" square out of each bottom corner of the layered unit as shown in Figure 6.

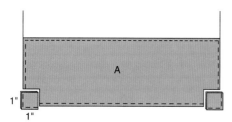

Figure 6

8. Align the B ruffle with gathered ends with the bottom edge of the 3¾" x 12" A rectangle; adjust ruffle width if needed. Pin and then baste layers together across top edge. Stitch layers together ⅜" from edge as shown in Figure 7. **Note:** *The gathered ends of this B strip should be above the cutout corners by at least ½" as shown in Figure 8.*

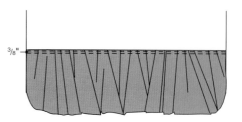

Figure 7

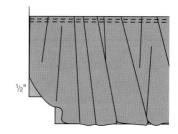

Figure 8

9. Place a second A strip right sides together on top of the stitched ruffle and stitch in place using a ⅜" seam allowance as shown in Figure 9.

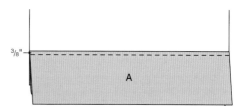

Figure 9

10. Press the A strip to the right side and topstitch ¼" above seam as shown in Figure 10.

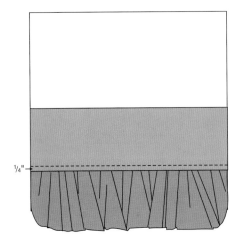

Figure 10

11. Repeat steps 8–10 with the remaining A and B strips to cover the interfacing rectangle as shown in Figure 11. **Note:** *Consecutive ruffles overlap previous ruffle to cover seams.*

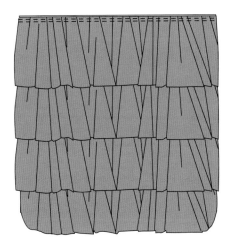

Figure 11

COMPLETING THE BAG

1. Place a C rectangle right side down on the second 12" x 13" interfacing rectangle and pin layers together and then baste to hold for bag back; cut out 1" squares on bottom corners as in step 7 of Completing the Bag Front.

2. Layer the pinned bag back right sides together with the ruffled bag front matching raw edges and cutout corners, making sure the ruffle edges are flat and included in the seams at the sides. Pin the edge of the bottom ruffle up to avoid stitching it into the bottom seam as shown in Figure 12. **Note:** *Gathered edge of bottom ruffle should be pinned in place at least ½" above cutout corners as shown in Figure 12.*

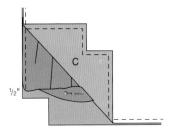

Figure 12

3. Sew side and bottom edges using a ⅜" seam allowance as shown in Figure 13; do not stitch the cutout corners.

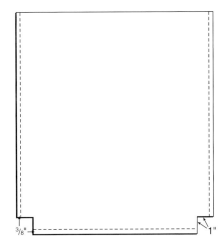

Figure 13

4. Flatten the bottom of the bag and pin the 1" cutout at one corner with side and bottom seams aligned; stitch a ⅜" seam as shown in Figure 14, being careful not to catch the ruffle in the seam.

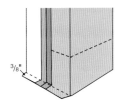

Figure 14

5. Repeat step 4 with the opposite corner cutout to make a flat bottom on the bag. Turn the bag right side out.

6. Layer the two inside pocket rectangles right sides together; sew along the two long edges using a ¼" seam allowance. Turn right side out and press flat. Topstitch along one long edge to complete the inside pocket.

7. Pin the inside pocket with the topstitched edge 5" down from one 12" edge on one of the remaining C rectangles and stitch in place across the bottom edge of the pocket as shown in Figure 15.

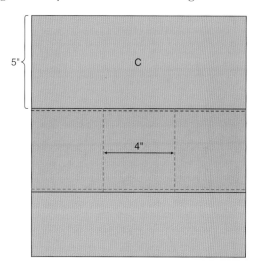

Figure 15

8. Divide the inside pocket into three 4" sections and stitch, again referring to Figure 15.

9. Place the C/pocket rectangle right sides together with the remaining C rectangle and cut a 1" square out of the bottom corners as in step 7 of Completing the Bag Front.

10. Stitch the side and bottom edges together using a ½" seam allowance.

11. Flatten and stitch bottom corners as in step 4 to complete the lining; do not turn right side out.

12. Join two strap strips on the short ends to make a long strip; press. Trim the strip to 50" long.

13. Fold the strip in half along length and press. Unfold and fold in the long raw edges to the centerfold and press as shown in Figure 16.

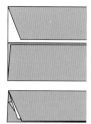

Figure 16

14. Tuck the 1¼" x 50" piece of interfacing inside the folds of the strip, again referring to Figure 16; refold in half and pin to hold.

15. Sew along both long edges using a ⅛" seam allowance to complete the strap.

16. Insert lining inside the outer bag with wrong sides together, aligning top edges; pin and baste to hold.

17. Center ends of strap over side seams as shown in Figure 17; baste to hold.

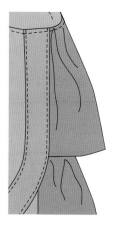

Figure 17

18. Join the binding strip on the short ends to make a tube. Fold the tube in half with wrong sides together and press to make a double-layered tube.

19. Pin the binding tube to the outside edge of the bag, matching raw edges; sew all around using a ⅜" seam allowance.

20. Turn the binding over the seam and to the inside of the bag and hand-stitch in place to cover top raw edge as shown in Figure 18 to finish the bag. ●

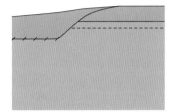

Figure 18

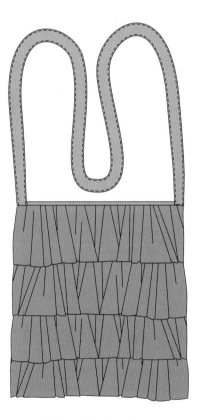

Hippy Swing Bag
Placement Diagram 9¼" x 11⅝" x 2"
(excluding strap)

Fun Folded Flap Bag

This handy assortment of bags would make perfect make-ahead gifts. Make a set for each person on your gift list and get started on the holidays cleaning out your fabric stash as you go.

Design by Missy Shepler

Skill Level
Confident Beginner

Finished Size
Bag Sizes: 7" x 8¾", 7" x 9¾" and 3½" x 5¾"

MATERIALS

- 2 coordinating fat quarters for each bag (any size)
- 9" x 21" rectangle batting
- Thread
- Basic sewing tools and supplies

CUTTING

From fat quarter 1:
- Cut 2 (2" x 21") strips for shoulder straps.

From fat quarter 2:
- Cut 2 (2¼" x 21") binding strips.

ASSEMBLY

1. Join the two 2" x 21" strips on the short ends to make a long strip; press seam open.
2. Press both short ends of the long strip ¼" to the wrong side. Fold the strip in half with wrong sides together along the length and press to crease the center of the strip.
3. Open the pressed strip and fold the two long edges to the center fold as shown in Figure 1; press again.

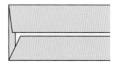

Figure 1

4. Refold the strip along the center crease to enclose raw edges and make a ½"-wide shoulder strap; topstitch all around a scant ¼" from edge referring to Figure 2; press again.

Figure 2

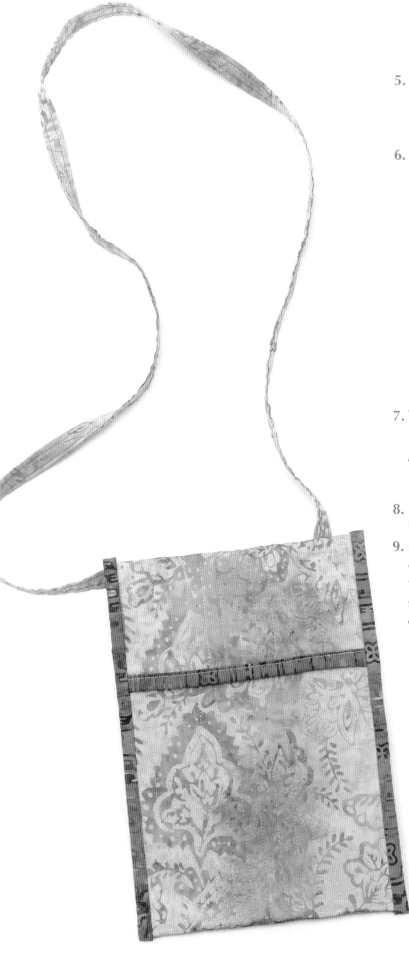

5. Lay the remainder of one fat quarter wrong side up on a flat surface; place the batting rectangle on top. Place the remainder of the second fat quarter right side up on top of the layers; pin layers together.

6. Quilt as desired. **Note:** *The samples were stitched in straight vertical lines about ½" apart as shown in Figure 3.*

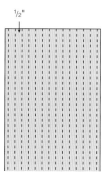

Figure 3

7. When quilting is complete, trim the quilted piece to 7" x 18". **Note:** *For the larger bag, trim the quilted piece to 7" x 20". For small bag, trim to make two 3½" x 12½" rectangles to get two small bags from the quilted rectangle.*

8. Fold each binding strip in half with wrong sides together along length and press.

9. Match one raw end of one strip to one short end of the 7" x 18" rectangle and stitch the binding to the lining side of the bag, matching raw edges as shown in Figure 4. Trim excess even with the edge of the rectangle.

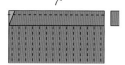

Figure 4

10. Fold the binding strip up and press flat. Fold the strip to the outside to enclose the seam and stitch the folded edge in place as shown in Figure 5.

Figure 5

11. Repeat steps 9 and 10 on the opposite short end of the rectangle to finish both ends.
12. On the outside of the bag rectangle, measure and mark handle attachment points 5½" from one short end and 1" from each side edge as shown in Figure 6. This will be the top of the bag.

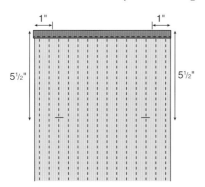

Figure 6

13. Pin the strap ends in place, making sure that the strap loops toward the top of the bag and is not twisted. Box-stitch the strap ends in place to secure the strap to the bag as shown in Figure 7.

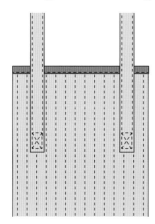

Figure 7

14. Fold the bag bottom up 7" from the bottom bound edge of the bag as shown in Figure 8; pin the bag together along both sides. ***Note:*** *For larger bag, fold bottom up 7½". For small bag, fold bottom up 4".*

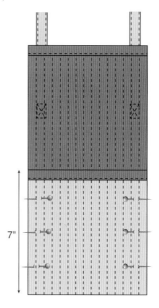

Figure 8

15. Fold the top bound edge of the bag down to overlap the bottom bound edge about ½" as shown in Figure 9; pin the bag together along both sides.

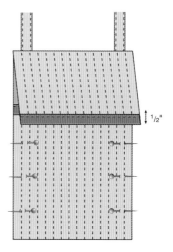

Figure 9

16. Pin, then sew both bag sides ⅛" from the edge as shown in Figure 10, making sure not to catch the shoulder straps in the stitching.

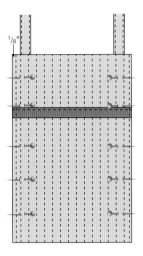

Figure 10

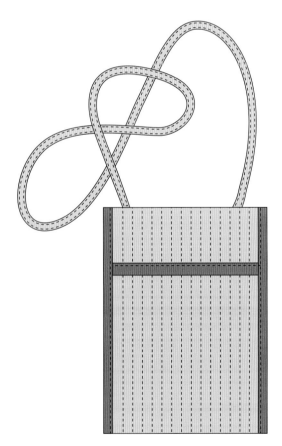

Fun Folded Flap Bag
Placement Diagram
7" x 8¾"

17. Cut two lengths of binding the length of the bag sides plus 1".

18. Unfold each short end of the binding strip and press ½" to the wrong side at each short end referring to Figure 11.

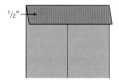

Figure 11

19. Refold the strip and press again.

20. Bind both sides of the bag as in steps 9 and 10 and hand-stitch each short end of each binding strip together to enclose side seams referring to Figure 12 to finish. ◗

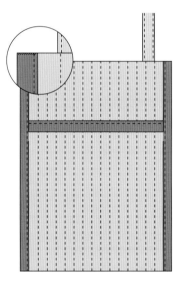

Figure 12

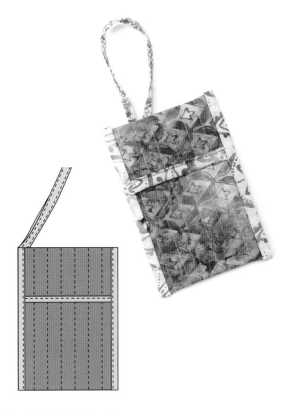

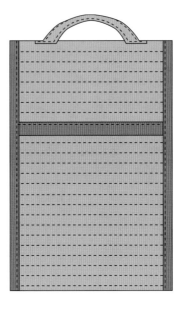

Fun Folded Flap Bag
Alternate Placement Diagram
3½" x 5¾"

Fun Folded Flap Bag
Alternate Placement Diagram
7" x 9¾"

Strap Options

There are many strap options from changing the length and width to placement of the straps. Here are two options you might consider. **Note:** Handles are attached to the bag before folding the bag ends or binding the sides.

Option 1: *Substitute a short handle instead of a long shoulder strap. The orange/pink sample bag has this type of strap.*

1. *Cut one 4" x 10" rectangle from either fabric. Press both short ends of the handle ½" to the wrong side.*

2. *Fold the handle in half with wrong sides together along length. Press the fold and open the pressed strip.*

3. *Fold the two long edges to the center fold and press again. Refold the handle along the center crease, enclosing raw edges, to make a handle 1" wide.*

4. *Stitch along both long edges to secure.*

5. *Fold each end of the handle strip under 1" to make double-layered ends. Pin each double-layer end 2" from the center, ½" from each side edge and 3½" from the top bound edge on the outside of the bag as shown in Figure A. Box-stitch the double-layer ends in place, again referring to Figure A.*

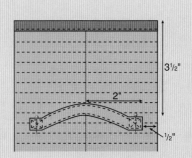

Figure A

Option 2: *For small bags, substitute a short loop or wrist strap instead of a strap or handle.*

1. *Cut a rectangle 2" by twice the desired strap length plus 1" and refer to steps 2–4 of Assembly to prepare the strap, except do not fold in the short ends.*

2. *Fold the prepared strap in half to make a loop and anchor the raw ends of the loop 2¼" from the top bound edge on one side edge of the outside of the bag referring to Figure B.*

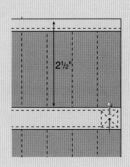

Figure B

New Narrows Tote

Turn 1" strips and a quilt-as-you-go technique into this trendy tote.

Design by Missy Shepler

Skill Level
Confident Beginner

Finished Size
Tote Size: Approximately 12" x 16" x 4"

CUTTING

From batik scraps:
- Cut 74 (1" x 20") strips.
- Cut 6 (2" x 42") strips for straps.

From coordinating batik:
- Cut 2 (16½" by fabric width) strips.
  Subcut each strip into 1 (16½" x 23") lining rectangle and 1 (16½" x 12½") inside pocket rectangle.

PREPARING THE STRAPS
1. Press both short ends of one strap strip ¼" to the wrong side. Fold the strap strip in half with wrong sides together along length; press to make a crease in the center of the strip.
2. Unfold the pressed strip and fold the two long edges to the center creased line on the wrong side of the strip as shown in Figure 1; press again.

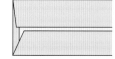

Figure 1

3. Referring to Figure 2, refold the strip along the center crease, enclosing the raw edges, to make a ½"-wide strip; stitch along both long edges to secure. **Note:** *You may stitch through the center of the strip using a decorative machine stitch if desired, referring to Figure 3.*

Figure 2

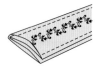

Figure 3

4. Repeat steps 1–3 to prepare a total of six straps.

COMPLETING THE OUTER BAG

1. Place one 1" x 20" strip right side up on one batting rectangle aligning the strip with the long 20" left edge of the batting as shown in Figure 4.

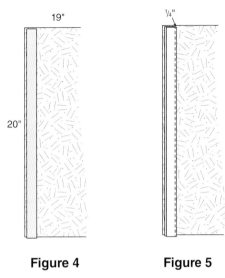

Figure 4   **Figure 5**

2. Place a second strip right side down on top of the first strip. Pin, then sew the strip to the batting ¼" from the right edge of the stacked strips as shown in Figure 5.

3. Flip the top strip to the right side and press as shown in Figure 6.

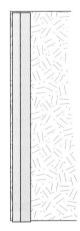

Figure 6

4. Continue adding strips until the entire piece of batting is covered to complete one outer bag panel.

5. Repeat steps 1–4 with the second batting rectangle and remaining 1"-wide strips to complete a second outer bag panel.

6. Trim both outer bag panels to 17" x 18½" with the sewn strips parallel with the 18½" measurement as shown in Figure 7.

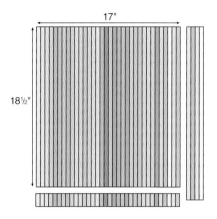

Figure 7

7. With right sides together, stitch the side and bottom seams of the outer bag panels together using a ⅜" seam allowance; press seams open.

8. Pinch the bag bottom and side together at one bottom corner, aligning seams, to form a triangle of fabric as shown in Figure 8.

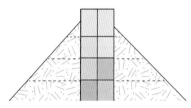

Figure 8

9. Measure down 2" from the point of the triangle and draw a line perpendicular to the seam as shown in Figure 9.

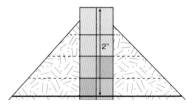

Figure 9

10. Stitch on the marked line to make a 4" bag bottom as shown in Figure 10. Stitch a second line ¼" away from the first seam closer to the triangle point to reinforce the seam.

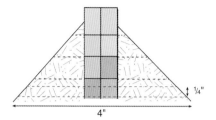

Figure 10

11. Trim the triangle point ¼" away from the last line of stitching referring to Figure 11; finger-press seam toward the bag bottom.

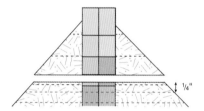

Figure 11

12. Repeat steps 8–11 on the opposite bottom corner.
13. Turn the outer bag right side out.

MAKING THE LINING

1. Make a double-fold hem along one long edge of each pocket rectangle by pressing under ¼" twice, then edgestitch the folded edge in place. **Note:** *If you prefer not to use stabilizer, work steps 2 and 3 omitting the stabilizer.*
2. Layer one 16½" x 23" lining rectangle right side up on one piece of stabilizer, aligning the two pieces along one 16½" edge. **Note:** *This will be the bottom. The lining will extend past the upper edge of the stabilizer.*
3. Place one pocket rectangle right side up on top of the lining, matching the bottom and side edges with the hemmed edge of the pocket toward the top. Pin, and then stitch the layers together around the side and bottom edges ⅛" from the raw edges referring to Figure 12.

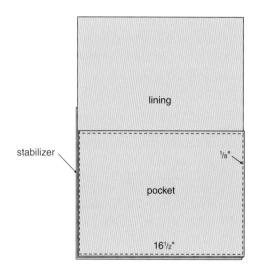

Figure 12

4. Measure and mark guidelines 2¼" from each side and along the bottom of the lining panel. Stitch along the marked lines, sewing through all layers to complete the lining panel referring to Figure 13. Add extra lines of stitching to subdivide the main pocket, if desired.

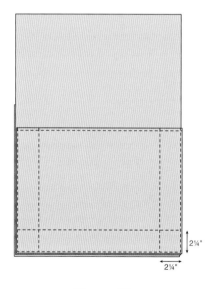

Figure 13

5. Repeat steps 2–4 to complete a second lining panel.
6. With right sides together, stitch the side and bottom seams of the lining panels together; press seams open.
7. Repeat steps 8–11 of Completing the Outer Bag to complete the lining. Do not turn right side out.

COMPLETING THE TOTE

1. Measure and mark handle placement lines 6" and 10" from the top edge of the outer bag along each side seam as shown in Figure 14.

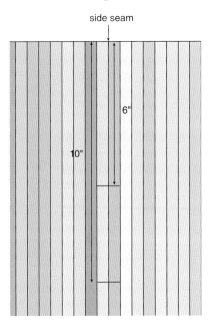

Figure 14

2. Layer and pin two prepared straps together, matching ends. Pin the paired straps in place with one set of matched ends on the 10" marked line and the straps centered on bag side seam as shown in Figure 15.

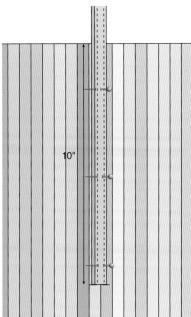

Figure 15

3. Sew the straps in place at the 6" marked line, leaving 4" tails as shown in Figure 16. Backstitch several times to secure.

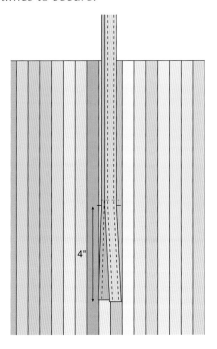

Figure 16

4. Repeat steps 2 and 3 with remaining straps, placing the additional two pairs on either side of the first pair, and secure in place.

5. Tie overhand knots in the loose tails close to the bag to hide the stitching as shown in Figure 17.

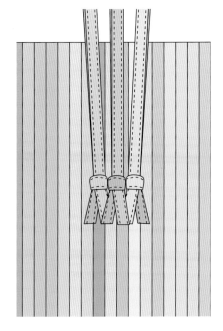

Figure 17

6. Tie several overhand knots to tie the straps together at various points to make it easier to grip referring to Figure 18 and the Placement Diagram.

Figure 18

7. Turn straps so they are not twisted at the opposite ends and repeat steps 3–5 to attach the remaining strap ends to the other side of the outer bag.
8. With wrong sides together, tuck the lining inside the outer bag, matching side and bottom seams. ***Note:*** *The lining will extend above the top of the outer bag.* Pin the lining to the outer bag.
9. Mark a center point on the bag front 1"–2" below the top edge of the outer bag as shown in Figure 19.

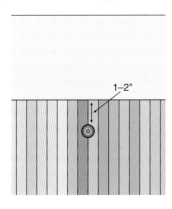

Figure 19

10. Follow manufacturer's instructions to insert one side of the magnetic snap on the bag front and the remaining side of the snap on the bag back.
11. Fold the straps down and out of the way, press the upper edge of the lining ½" to the wrong side and fold over the top of the outer bag with the lining covering about 4" of the outer bag as shown in Figure 20.

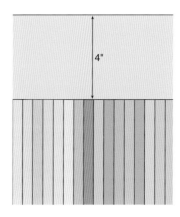

Figure 20

12. Pin, and then stitch the lining to the outer bag along the folded edge using a decorative machine stitch referring to Figure 21 to finish. ●

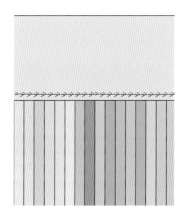

Figure 21

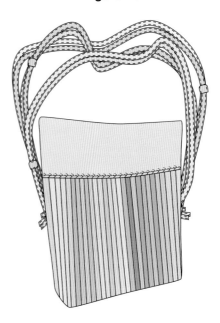

New Narrows Tote
Placement Diagram Approximately 12 x 16" x 4"

Brown Baggin' It

Save the planet while lunching in style. Laminated cotton makes this bag spill-safe and durable.

Design by Carol Zentgraf

Skill Level
Intermediate

Finished Size
Bag Size: 6½" x 9" x 4"

MATERIALS

- Assorted 45"-wide laminated cotton print fabrics to equal ¾ yard
- ½ yard coordinating laminated cotton print fabric
- Thread
- 6¼" length hook-and-loop tape
- Self-adhesive, double-sided basting tape
- Basic sewing tools and supplies

Project Note: *Use a ½" seam allowance and sew seams with right sides together unless otherwise noted. To avoid mistakes when stitching the laminated bag, make a muslin sample first using a 7½" x 30½" piece for the outer shell and two K pieces as listed in the cutting chart.*

CUTTING

From assorted laminated cotton prints:
- Cut 1 each 2½" x 5" A, 4½" x 5" B, 4" x 5" C, 6" x 5" D, 4" x 5" F, 8" x 5" G, 3½" x 5" H rectangles, 5" E square and 1½" x 30½" J strip.
- Cut 2 (5" x 10") K strips.

From coordinating laminated cotton print:
- Cut 2 (7½" x 10") front and back lining piece, 2 (5" x 10") lining side panels and 1 (5" x 7½") lining bottom.

ASSEMBLY

1. Join the A–H pieces in alphabetical order along the 5" sides as shown in Figure 1; finger-press seams toward H and topstitch in place, again referring to Figure 1. Add I, and then J to the long side of the right-side edge, again referring to Figure 1.

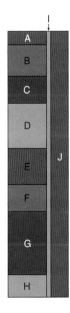

Figure 1

2. Fold one short edge of each K side panel under ½" and secure with basting tape.
3. Repeat step 2 on the top A short edge of the pieced panel.

4. With the folded edges aligned, sew the K side panel, stopping stitching ½" from the lower corner as shown in Figure 2. Clip the pieced panel and K at the bottom corner, again referring to Figure 2.

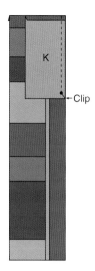

Figure 2

5. Align the edge of the pieced panel with the bottom edge of K and stitch across, beginning and ending ½" from corners as shown in Figure 3; clip corner.

Figure 3

6. Stitch up remaining long edge of K to outside edge as shown in Figure 4.

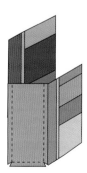

Figure 4

7. Repeat steps 4–6 with remaining K piece on the opposite long edge of the pieced panel.

8. To make the flap, fold 4" of the remainder of the pieced panel under with right sides together as shown in Figure 5. Sew the sides together, stopping the stitching at the top of the side panels. Trim the seam allowances, clip corners and turn the flap right side out.

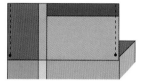

Figure 5

9. Sew the hook strip of the hook-and-loop tape to the inside of the flap close to the top edge as shown in Figure 6.

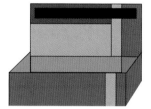

Figure 6

10. To make the lining, sew the long edges of the lining side panels to the long edges of the front and back lining panels to make a box shape. Sew the bottom to the box shape to complete the lining; do not turn right side out. Turn the top edges of the lining to the wrong side ½" and secure with basting tape.

11. Place the lining inside the bag with seams matching and upper edges even and covering the raw edge of the flap. Stitch the lining and bag edges together; continue the stitching across the back top edge of the lining to secure the flap.

12. Fold the flap down and mark the position for the loop tape strip. Sew the strip in place. ●

Tips for Sewing Laminated Fabrics

• *Needle or pin holes will show on laminated fabrics. Avoid ripping seams and use self-adhesive, double-sided basting tape instead of pins.*

• *Do not touch a hot iron to the laminated side of the fabric. If pressing is necessary, use an iron on the lowest setting and press on the wrong side of the fabric only. For best results, finger-press seams and edges.*

• *Finger-press seam allowances to one side and stitch in place instead of pressing them open. This increases the water resistance of the finished project.*

• *Use a sharp needle in your machine. A size 12 was used to stitch the sample.*

• *Using a Teflon foot on your machine is helpful when sewing on this type of fabric.*

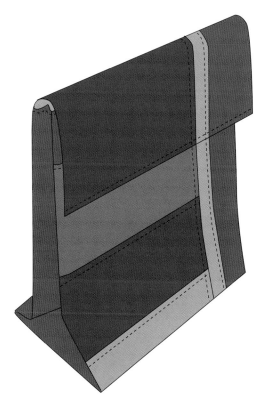

Brown Baggin' It
Placement Diagram 6½" x 9" x 4"

Grocery Tote

Fill and reuse this large insulated tote on all your shopping trips to do your part in the "Go Green" movement.

Design by Carolyn S. Vagts for The Village Pattern Company

Skill Level
Beginner

Finished Size
Bag Size: 20" x 15" x 8"

CUTTING

From print 3:
- Cut 1 (3½" by fabric width) C strip.
- Cut 2 (2¼" by fabric width) binding strips.

PREPARING QUILTED PIECES
1. Sandwich the insulated batting between the coordinating prints 1 and 2; quilt as desired by hand or machine.

2. Cut the following from the quilted fabric: two 20½" x 19½" rectangles for tote front and back pieces; one 12" x 9" rectangle for flap; and one 13½" x 9½" rectangle for pocket.

COMPLETING THE TOTE
1. Cut a 4" square from each bottom corner of the tote front and back pieces as shown in Figure 1.
2. Fold each binding strip in half with wrong sides together along the length; press. Set one folded strip aside to bind the flap.

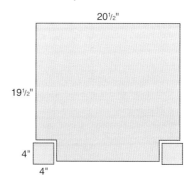

Figure 1

3. Cut a 9½" length from the second binding strip.
4. With raw edges even, sew binding strip across the top front edge of the quilted pocket square; press binding up and turn to the back side; slipstitch binding edge in place. **Note:** *The pocket front should be the fabric that will be inside the tote.*

5. Center the pocket right side up on the quilted front, aligning at bottom edge as shown in Figure 2; stitch across bottom edge to hold. Pin top of pocket in place.

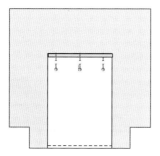

Figure 2

6. Cut two 54" lengths nylon belting for straps.
7. Pin one strap piece on the tote front with ends of strap even with bottom edges of tote, overlapping pocket edges at least ½" as shown in Figure 3; topstitch edges of strap in place on pocket edges, again referring to Figure 3, double-stitching at top edge of pocket to reinforce.

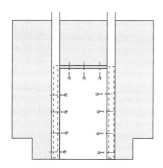

Figure 3

8. Using the stitched front piece as a guide for placement, pin and stitch the second strap pieces to the back side of the tote referring to Figure 4.

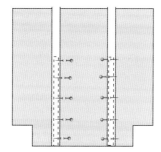

Figure 4

9. Sew tote front to tote back right sides together along tote side and bottom edges as shown in Figure 5; do not stitch corner edges. Finish seam edges as desired.

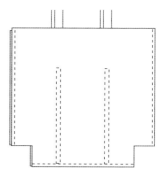

Figure 5

10. Flatten bottom of bag so bottom seam matches side seams and sew raw edges together to make a box bottom on the tote as shown in Figure 6; repeat for second side. Finish seam edges as desired.

Figure 6

11. Beginning at the end of one 9" side of the flap piece and referring to step 4, sew the reserved binding strip to one short side, stopping stitching ¼" from the first corner; sew to the corner point at a 45-degree angle as shown in Figure 7.

Figure 7

12. Flip binding strip up and away from the flap, and then fold it back into place along the next side to be stitched as shown in Figure 8. ***Note:*** *Fold should be even with the first side stitched.* Continue

stitching binding around edges of flap, mitering the next corner in the same manner, and leaving one 12" edge unbound. Fold binding to the back side; hand-stitch in place.

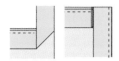

Figure 8

13. Place flap inside tote, centered on upper edge of back with lining fabrics together and raw edges even as shown in Figure 9; stitch across top edge.

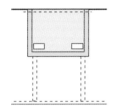

Figure 9

14. Cut the hook-and-loop tape in half; sew hook pieces to lower corners of the flap on top outer side, again referring to Figure 9. Sew loop pieces to the upper inside edge of tote front to match with hook pieces on flap.

15. Measure around top edge of tote; add 1" to the measurement. Cut the 3½" C strip to this size to make top band. Press under ½" on the beginning end and along one long edge.

16. Pin and stitch the C strip to the inside edge of the bag with raw edges even, starting at one side seam with the folded end and overlapping unpressed end on folded end to finish.

17. Turn the C strip to the right side of the bag, with folded edge over raw edge; press and topstitch the C piece in place on the outside of the bag and at the overlapping edge at the side to finish. ●

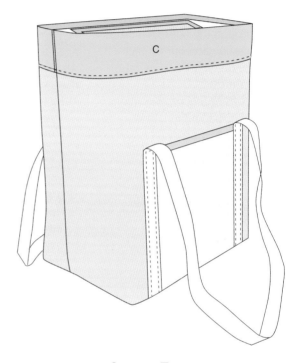

Grocery Tote
Placement Diagram 20" x 15" x 8"

Quilting Basics

The following is a reference guide. For more information, consult a comprehensive quilting book.

ALWAYS:

- Read through the entire pattern before you begin your project.
- Purchase quality, 100 percent cotton fabrics.
- When considering prewashing, do so with ALL of the fabrics being used. Generally, prewashing is not required in quilting.
- Use ¼" seam allowance for all stitching unless otherwise instructed.
- Use a short-to-medium stitch length.
- Make sure your seams are accurate.

QUILTING TOOLS & SUPPLIES

- Rotary cutter and mat
- Scissors for paper and fabric
- Nonslip quilting rulers
- Marking tools
- Sewing machine
- Sewing machine feet:
- ¼" seaming foot (for piecing)
- Walking or even-feed foot (for piecing or quilting)
- Darning or free-motion foot (for free-motion quilting)
- Quilting hand-sewing needles
- Straight pins
- Curved safety pins for basting
- Seam ripper
- Iron and ironing surface

BASIC TECHNIQUES
Appliqué
FUSIBLE APPLIQUÉ

All templates are reversed for use with this technique.

1. Trace the instructed number of templates ¼" apart onto the paper side of paper-backed fusible web. Cut apart the templates, leaving a margin around each, and fuse to the wrong side of the fabric following fusible web manufacturer's instructions.
2. Cut the appliqué pieces out on the traced lines, remove paper backing and fuse to the background referring to the appliqué motif given.
3. Finish appliqué raw edges with a straight, satin, blanket, zigzag or blind-hem machine stitch with matching or invisible thread.

TURNED-EDGE APPLIQUÉ

1. Trace the printed reversed templates onto template plastic. Flip the template over and mark as the right side.
2. Position the template, right side up, on the right side of fabric and lightly trace, spacing images ½" apart. Cut apart, leaving a ¼" margin around the traced lines.
3. Clip curves and press edges ¼" to the wrong side around the appliqué shape.
4. Referring to the appliqué motif, pin or baste appliqué shapes to the background.
5. Hand-stitch shapes in place using a blind stitch and thread to match or machine-stitch using a short blind hemstitch and either matching or invisible thread.

Borders

Most patterns give an exact size to cut borders. You may check those sizes by comparing them to the horizontal and vertical center measurements of your quilt top.

STRAIGHT BORDERS

1. Mark the centers of the side borders and quilt top sides.
2. Stitch borders to quilt top sides with right sides together and matching raw edges and center marks using a ¼" seam. Press seams toward borders.
3. Repeat with top and bottom border lengths.

MITERED BORDERS

1. Add at least twice the border width to the border lengths instructed to cut.
2. Center and sew the side borders to the quilt, beginning and ending stitching ¼" from the quilt corner and backstitching (Figure 1). Repeat with the top and bottom borders.

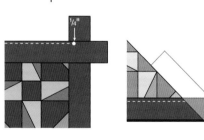

Figure 1   **Figure 2**

3. Fold and pin quilt right sides together at a 45-degree angle on one corner (Figure 2). Place a straightedge along the fold and lightly mark a line across the border ends.

4. Stitch along the line, backstitching to secure. Trim seam to ¼" and press open (Figure 3).

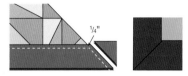

Figure 3

Quilt Backing & Batting

We suggest that you cut your backing and batting 8" larger than the finished quilt-top size. If preparing the backing from standard-width fabrics, remove the selvages and sew two or three lengths together; press seams open. If using 108"-wide fabric, trim to size on the straight grain of the fabric.

Prepare batting the same size as your backing. You can purchase prepackaged sizes or battings by the yard and trim to size.

Quilting

1. Press quilt top on both sides and trim all loose threads.
2. Make a quilt sandwich by layering the backing right side down, batting and quilt top centered right side up on flat surface and smooth out. Pin or baste layers together to hold.
3. Mark quilting design on quilt top and quilt as desired by hand or machine. *Note: If you are sending your quilt to a professional quilter, contact them for specifics about preparing your quilt for quilting.*
4. When quilting is complete, remove pins or basting. Trim batting and backing edges even with raw edges of quilt top.

Binding the Quilt

1. Join binding strips on short ends with diagonal seams to make one long strip; trim seams to ¼" and press seams open (Figure 4).

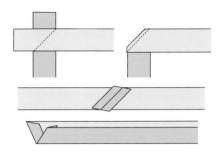

Figure 4

2. Fold 1" of one short end to wrong side and press. Fold the binding strip in half with wrong sides together along length, again referring to Figure 4; press.
3. Starting about 3" from the folded short end, sew binding to quilt top edges, matching raw edges and using a ¼" seam. Stop stitching ¼" from corner and backstitch (Figure 5).

Stop ¼"

Figure 5

4. Fold binding up at a 45-degree angle to seam and then down even with quilt edges, forming a pleat at corner, referring to Figure 6.

Figure 6

5. Resume stitching from corner edge as shown in Figure 6, down quilt side, backstitching ¼" from next corner. Repeat, mitering all corners, stitching to within 3" of starting point.
6. Trim binding end long enough to tuck inside starting end and complete stitching (Figure 7).

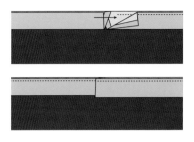

Figure 7

7. Fold binding to quilt back and stitch in place by hand or machine to complete your quilt.

QUILTING TERMS

- **Appliqué:** Adding fabric motifs to a foundation fabric by hand or machine (see Appliqué section of Basic Techniques).
- **Basting:** This temporarily secures layers of quilting materials together with safety pins, thread or a spray adhesive in preparation for quilting the layers.

  Use a long, straight stitch to hand- or machine-stitch one element to another holding the elements in place during construction and usually removed after construction.
- **Batting:** An insulating material made in a variety of fiber contents that is used between the quilt top and back to provide extra warmth and loft.
- **Binding:** A finishing strip of fabric sewn to the outer raw edges of a quilt to cover them.

  Straight-grain binding strips, cut on the crosswise straight grain of the fabric (see Straight & Bias Grain Lines illustration on the next page), are commonly used.

  Bias binding strips are cut at a 45-degree angle to the straight grain of the fabric. They are used when binding is being added to curved edges.
- **Block:** The basic quilting unit that is repeated to complete the quilt's design composition. Blocks can be pieced, appliquéd or solid and are usually square or rectangular in shape.
- **Border:** The frame of a quilt's central design used to visually complete the design and give the eye a place to rest.

- **Fabric Grain:** The fibers that run either parallel (lengthwise grain) or perpendicular (crosswise grain) to the fabric selvage are straight grain.

   Bias is any diagonal line between the lengthwise or crosswise grain. At these angles the fabric is less stable and stretches easily. The true bias of a woven fabric is a 45-degree angle between the lengthwise and crosswise grain lines.

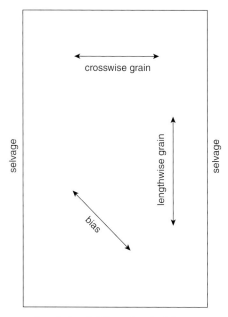

Straight & Bias Grain Lines

- **Mitered Corners:** Matching borders or turning bindings at a 45-degree angle at corners.
- **Patchwork:** A general term for the completed blocks or quilts that are made from smaller shapes sewn together.
- **Pattern:** This may refer to the design of a fabric or to the written instructions for a particular quilt design.
- **Piecing:** The act of sewing smaller pieces and/or units of a block or quilt together.

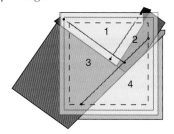

Foundation Piecing

Paper or foundation piecing is sewing fabric to a paper or cloth foundation in a certain order.

String or chain piecing is sewing pieces together in a continuous string without clipping threads between sections.

String or Chain Piecing

Pressing: Pressing is the process of placing the iron on the fabric, lifting it off the fabric and placing it down in another location to flatten seams or crease fabric without sliding the iron across the fabric.

   Quilters do not usually use steam when pressing, since it can easily distort fabric shapes.

   Generally, seam allowances are pressed toward the darker fabric in quilting so that they do not show through the lighter fabric.

   Seams are pressed in opposite directions where seams are being joined to allow seams to butt against each other and to distribute bulk.

   Seams are pressed open when multiple seams come together in one place.

   If you have a question about pressing direction, consult a comprehensive quilting guide for guidance.

- **Quilt (noun):** A sandwich of two layers of fabric with a third insulating material between them that is then stitched together with the edges covered or bound.
- **Quilt (verb):** Stitching several layers of fabric materials together with a decorative design. Stippling, crosshatch, channel, in-the-ditch, free-motion, allover and meandering are all terms for quilting designs.

Meandering

Stitch in the ditch

Channel

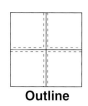
Outline

- **Quilt Sandwich:** A layer of insulating material between a quilt's top and back fabric.
- **Rotary Cutting:** Using a rotary cutting blade and straightedge to cut fabric.
- **Sashing:** Strips of fabric sewn between blocks to separate or set off the designs.
- **Subcut:** A second cutting of rotary-cut strips that makes the basic shapes used in block and quilt construction.
- **Template:** A pattern made from a sturdy material which is then used to cut shapes for patchwork and appliqué quilting.

QUILTING SKILL LEVELS

- **Beginner:** A quilter who has been introduced to the basics of cutting, piecing and assembling a quilt top and is working to master these skills. Someone who has the knowledge of how to sandwich, quilt and bind a quilt, but may not have necessarily accomplished the task yet.
- **Confident Beginner:** A quilter who has pieced and assembled several quilt tops and is comfortable with the process, and is now ready to move on to more challenging techniques and projects using at least two different techniques.
- **Intermediate:** A quilter who is comfortable with most quilting techniques and has a good understanding for design, color and the whole process. A quilter who is experienced in paper piecing, bias piecing and projects involving multiple techniques. Someone who is confident in making fabric selections other than those listed in the pattern.
- **Advanced:** A quilter who is looking for a challenging design. Someone who knows she or he can make any type of quilt. Someone who has the skills to read, comprehend and complete a pattern, and is willing to take on any technique. A quilter who is comfortable in her or his skills and has the ability to select fabric suited to the project. ●